As you begin this 31-day journal, I pray that God opens your eyes so you will begin to see something new, I hope it opens your ears to hear his voice and your heart to receive what he has for you. It's never too late to RESTART!

These next 31 days will remind you of how equipped you really are. Every day is a new day, and we must get ready to enjoy it. There's a new journey waiting for you, but you must begin to Remove, Reclaim, Reflect, and the many other Re words that you will begin to discover in the 31 Days of Re.

Now it's time to flip the page and hit the RESTART button!

Your time is now, YOU GOT THIS!

Sincerely,

Jabrina Speaks

31 Days of Re Daily Devotion:

Copyright © 2020 Jabrina Thompson

All rights reserved. This book or any portion thereof may not be reproduced or used in any manner whatsoever without the express written permission of the author except for the use of brief quotations in a book review. Printed in the United States of America Book

First Printing
ISBN 978-1-943284-88-7 pbk
ISBN 978-1-943284-52-8 ebk

A2Z Books Publishing Lithonia, GA 30058 www.A2ZBooksPublishing.net Manufactured in the United States of America A2Z Books Publishing has allowed this work to remain exactly as the Publisher & Author Intended.

Dedication

This book is dedicated to my late father Henry "Wallace" Thompson. He was not just my father but he was my daddy, friend, business partner, and king. I am forever grateful to have had a father like him.

Forever his Jabrina #DADDYSGIRL

Acknowledgement

First, I would like to tell God Thank you!

I would like to thank my parents Regina Thompson and my late father Henry Thompson for being amazing parents and making sure I understood that hard work pays off and what the true definition of love and support is.

To my sister Jamia Thompson and brother Jabin Robinson I love and appreciate you so much. Thanks for always answering the call.

To all of my family and very close friends, I love you! Jabrina Speaks is here because you've always helped, supported and showed nothing but love.

And to you, my supporters and readers, this journal was written with you in mind. Thank you for believing in Jabrina Speaks.

Philippians 4:13 I can do all this through him who gives me strength.

Contents

Dedication 3
Acknowledgement 4
Day 1 Restart 6
Day 2 Resolve 8
Day 3 Reintroduce 10
Day 4 Relax 12
Day 5 Rejoice 14
Day 6 Responsible 16
Day 7 Restore 18
Day 8 Relationship(s) 20
Day 9 Release 22
Day 10 Rebuild 24
Day 11 Redirect 26
Day 12 Resuscitate 28
Day 13 Recreate 30
Day 14 Reconsider 32
Day 15 Reassess 34
Day 16 Relove 36
Day 17 Recover 38
Day 18 Realign/ Realignment 40
Day 19 Regroup 42
Day 20 Reject 44
Day 21 Remind 46
Day 22 Renew/Refresh 48
Day 23 Require 50
Day 24 Reap 52
Day 25 Regrets 54
Day 26 Reach 56
Day 27 Recharge 58
Day 28 Remove 60
Day 29 Rethink, Respond and Retaliate 62
Day 30 Resilience/ Reaffirm 64
Day 31 Reflect, Review and Reinforce 66

What do you need to RESTART?

Day 1 Restart

Definition: 1. Start again 2. New start or beginning.

It's time to RESTART something! Think about where you are in life right now, and let's start again. It is not too late to begin something new. Whether it is a new career, new relationships, or new goals, it is okay to RESTART today!

What are you restarting today, and why?

_____
_____
_____
_____
_____
_____
_____
_____
_____
_____

Jeremiah 29:11 For I know the plans I have for you," declares the LORD, "plans to prosper you and not to harm you, plans to give you hope and a future.

What do you need to RESOLVE?

Day 2 Resolve

Definition: 1. Settle or find a solution to (a problem, dispute, or contentious matter) 2. Firm determination to do something.

Today I would like you to think about what needs to be resolved. Some of us have problems that we have allowed to linger too long, and now it's time to RESOLVE them. The definition tells us that it is to find a solution or firm determination. I want you to be determined on your next move, no longer being a problem but resolving it so you can take your next step. Think about it.

_____

_____

_____

_____

_____

_____

_____

_____

_____

Psalm 112:8 His resolve is firm; he will not succumb to fear before he looks in triumph on his enemies.

It's time to REINTRODUCE yourself!

Day 3 Reintroduce

Definition: 1. bring (something, especially a law or system) into existence or effect again.

Allow me to reintroduce myself… and that's what many of you need to do today! It's time to Reintroduce YOU! Remind the world of your gifts and talents. Maybe you forgot who you really are. You were fearfully and wonderfully made. You got this and it's time to reintroduce yourself.

Hello my name is_____

and allow me to REINTRODUCE myself._____

> "If you know me based on who I was a year ago, you don't know me at all. My growth game is strong. Allow me to reintroduce myself."

Today it's time to RELAX!

Day 4 Relax

Definition: 1. make or become less tense or anxious.

Guess what? There are some things you won't be able to change, so today, I want you to RELAX! Leave it in God's hands. Take this day for you and your family and enjoy it. Go shopping, read a book, go to the beach but most definitely relax.

How are you going to relax today? What did you release while you were in a relaxed mood?

_____
_____
_____
_____
_____
_____
_____
_____
_____
_____
_____

John 14:27 Peace I leave with you; my peace I give you. I do not give to you as the world gives. Do not let your hearts be troubled and do not be afraid.

Let us REJOICE!

Day 5 Rejoice

Definition: 1. feel or show great joy or delight. 2. Cause joy to.

It's a new day and it's time to rejoice. Today is Day 5. What has brought you delight and joy? I want you to make a list of the things that bring you joy and rejoice in them. No longer being sad about where you are but being able to REJOICE in everything!

_____

_____

_____

_____

_____

_____

_____

_____

_____

_____

_____

_____

Psalm 118:24 This is the day which the Lord hath made; we will rejoice and be glad in it.

You must be RESPONSIBLE.

Day 6 Responsible

Definition: 1. Having an obligation to do something or having control over or care for someone, as part of one's job or role. **2.** Being the primary cause of something and so able to be blamed or credited for it.

Today let's be responsible for our actions, thoughts, and words. No longer blaming anyone but looking in the mirror and owning our own. What are you responsible for? What are your thoughts about the word responsible?

_____

_____

_____

_____

_____

_____

_____

_____

_____

_____

_____

Galatians 6:5 Each of you must take responsibility for doing the creative best you can with your own life.

It's time to RESTORE You!

Day 7 Restore

Definition: 1. To put or bring back into existence or use 2. To bring back to or put back into a former or original state: RENEW

It is time to restore you! Allowing yourself to open back up to love, friendships, good health, and life. All those things can be restored. Make a list of things that you would like to be restored and begin to work on them. Today is RESTORATION!

_____
_____
_____
_____
_____
_____
_____
_____
_____
_____
_____
_____
_____

Jeremiah 30:17 But I will restore you to health and heal your wounds' declares the LORD, 'because you are called an outcast, Zion for whom no one cares.'

Who are you connected with?

Day 8 Relationships

Definition: 1. The state of being related or interrelated studied the relationship between the variables. 2. The relation is connecting or binding participants in a relationship.

There's a saying, "It's not what you know, but who you know." Who are you connected with? Relationships are vital and they allow us to grow, mature, and learn who we are. Think about your previous and present relationships and how you've grown. These relationships are with family, friends, and significant others. Remember, on this journey we call life, people are only here for a season, reason, or a lifetime.

What relationship(s) did you allow to go on too long?

What are your feelings about relationships?

_____
_____
_____
_____
_____
_____
_____

> I believe forgiveness is the best form of love in any relationship. It takes a strong person to say they're sorry and an even stronger person to forgive. Yolanda Hadid

What do you need to RELEASE to be a better person?

Day 9 Release

Definition: 1. Allow or enable to escape from confinement; set free. 2 Allow (something) to move, act, or flow freely. 3. The action or process of releasing or being released.

Before you can move on to tomorrow, you need to RELEASE something today! Your release may be a pain, unforgiveness, betrayal, anger, or self-doubt, but whatever it is, you must let it go TODAY! You can't continue living in the past. Today I want you to RELEASE everything on this paper. Writing it all down and letting it go. There's something ahead waiting for you, but you must decide today to make a release.

_____
_____
_____
_____
_____
_____
_____
_____
_____
_____

John 8:32 "Then you will know the truth, and the truth will set you free."

One block at a time… REBUILD!

Day 10 Rebuild

Definition: 1. Build (something) again after it has been damaged or destroyed.

Our life is like building blocks, one step at a time. Each block representing something (family, children, job, love, and/or business), but unfortunately, in our day to day, these blocks may be destroyed. You may find yourself damaged, but today you can REBUILD! You have been given another opportunity to pick up a new block of life. Below write down your new blocks and what you're going to do to keep building them up. Let's get to work and begin to REBUILD!

_____
_____
_____
_____
_____
_____
_____
_____
_____
_____

2 Corinthians 5:1 - For we know that if our earthly house of [this] tabernacle were dissolved, we have a building of God, a house not made with hands, eternal in the heavens.

Your direction has changed.

Day 11 Redirect

Definition: 1. Direct (something) to a new or different place or purpose.

It is time to redirect your thoughts and actions. Redirecting comes with a new mindset. Though it may not always be easy to find positivity in a negative situation, it is your duty to begin to redirect any negative thoughts you are thinking at the moment.

How are you redirecting your thoughts and feelings on what's going on right now in your life?

_____
_____
_____
_____
_____
_____
_____
_____
_____
_____
_____
_____

"I can change the story. I am the story." – Jeanette Winterson

You will LIVE!

Day 12 Resuscitate

Definition: 1. Revive (someone) from unconsciousness or apparent death. 2. Make (something such as an idea or enterprise) active or vigorous again.

Some days we feel like giving up and throwing in the towel, but today is the day God **RESUSCITATES** you and your **PURPOSE**! Today you will **LIVE** and be **GREAT**! Today write down the things you are grateful for. Begin to think of the things that died or are trying to die and begin to **SPEAK LIFE** over them.

_____

_____

_____

_____

_____

_____

_____

_____

_____

_____

I SHALL NOT DIE

Psalm 118:17 - I will not die but live, and will proclaim what the LORD has done.

Pick up the pieces and recreate your steps!

Day 13 Recreate

Definition: 1. Create again 2. Reproduce; re-enact.

What do you need to recreate? How will you create it? It is time to refresh the things you've allowed to die or sit aside. It's okay to start over. Don't allow anyone to make you feel like there's no do-overs. Keep pushing forward and use today as your day to begin to RECREATE.

I would like to recreate _____

_____
_____
_____
_____
_____
_____
_____
_____
_____
_____
_____
_____

Isaiah 65:17 - For behold, I create new heavens and a new earth, and the former things shall not be remembered or come into mind.

Time waits for no one.

Day 14 Reconsider

Definition: 1. Consider (something) again, especially for a possible change of decision regarding it.

Life will have you reconsidering somethings. Relationships, Career, and maybe even life choices. The word reconsider gives us synonyms like readdress, reanalyze, redefine, reevaluate, reexamine, rethink, and revisit.

Reading each of those synonyms, where are you now with the word RECONSIDER? What's on your plate to reconsider?

_____
_____
_____
_____
_____
_____
_____
_____
_____
_____
_____

"Everything you can imagine is real." – Pablo Picasso

Are you going to pass the test?

Day 15 Reassess

Definition: 1. Consider or assess again, especially while paying attention to new or different factors.

In life, we must stop, think, and reassess. You must begin to ask yourself where am I, what am I doing here and of course the important one why am I here?

Go a little deeper and see if it brings you joy and peace? Or is it a liability or an asset?

Today, day 15… Stop and begin to reassess.

_____
_____
_____
_____
_____
_____
_____
_____
_____

"It is not until you change your identity to match your life blueprint that you will understand why everything in the past never worked."
– Shannon L. Alder

Learn to LOVE you again!

Day 16 Relove

Definition: 1. To love in return

When was the last time you loved yourself first? In life, we go on and on and forget how important it is to have self-love. When was the last time you showed yourself, unconditional love? How could you love yourself better?

_____

"True love stories never have endings." – Richard Bach

You shall RECOVER it ALL!

Day 17 Recover

Definition: 1. Return to a normal state of health, mind, or strength. 2. Find or regain possession of (something stolen or lost).

Today think about where you are and where you want to be. What do you need to recover to get there? Some of us are in the recovery room now from hurt, depression, anxiety, and other things that we thought would've taken us out, but God heard your cry and placed you in the recovery room. Think about what you've gained while you recovered.

"There's a blessing in the recovery room." – Jabrina Speaks

It's time to get straight!

Day 18 Realign/ Realignment

Definition: 1. Change or restore to a different or former position or state. 2. Change one's position or attitude with regard to (a person, organization, or cause).

Yes, you've made it to Day 18, and it's time to change your position, maybe your attitude, and anything that's holding you back from getting it straight. There's been a few places that need to be realigned but not reinvented.

What are they, and where are you now?

_____

_____

_____

_____

_____

_____

_____

_____

_____

_____

_____

DON'T REINVENT THE WHEEL, JUST REALIGN IT

ANTHONY J DANGELO
PICTUREQUOTES.com

"When you align yourself with God's purpose as described in the Scriptures, something special happens to your life." – Bono

Let's put it all back together.

Day 19 Regroup

Definition: 1. Reassemble or cause to reassemble into organized groups, typically after being attacked or defeated. 2. Rearrange (something) into a new group or groups.

You may have been attacked and even felt that you lost the race but today you will begin to REGROUP! Regroup your thoughts. Regroup your family. Regroup your peace! The race is not given to the swift. Reassemble every task. Make a list and get organized. YOU GOT THIS! It's time to regroup!

_____
_____
_____
_____
_____
_____
_____
_____
_____
_____

"We're always experiencing joy or sadness. But there are lots of people who've closed down. And there are times in one's life when one has to close down just to regroup."– Leonard Cohen

Rejection saved my life!

Day 20 Reject

Definition: 1. Dismiss as inadequate, inappropriate, or not to one's taste. 2. Refuse to agree to (a request).

At one time in your life you thought the rejection from your spouse, job, friends or family was the most devastating moments ever. You thought you did everything wrong, but today I am here to remind you that the rejection saved your life. You were able to find yourself on so many levels. Today, write down the rejections you thought would have taken you out and begin to make peace with them.

_____
_____
_____
_____
_____
_____
_____
_____
_____
_____
_____
_____

"Thank you for the rejection, and it saved my life!" – Jabrina Speaks

Remind them!

Day 21 Remind

Definition: 1. Cause (someone) to remember someone or something. 2. Bring something, especially a commitment or necessary course of action, to the attention of (someone).

Yep, remind them! Remind them of your love. Remind them of your uniqueness. Remind them of how special you are. Remind them of your gift. Remind them you're great. Guess what? "Them" is YOU! Remind yourself today!

_____

_____

_____

_____

_____

_____

_____

_____

BE WHO YOU ARE AND SAY WHAT YOU FEEL, BECAUSE THOSE WHO MIND DON'T MATTER AND THOSE WHO MATTER DON'T MIND.

"Remind yourself that the greatest technique for bringing peace into your life is always to choose being kind when you have a choice between being right or being kind." – Wayne Dryer

It's a NEW day.

Day 22 Renew/Refresh

Definition: 1. Resume (an activity) after an interruption. 2. Re-establish (a relationship).

Refresh 1. Give new strength or energy to; reinvigorate.

Smell the fresh air. Today is a new day for a fresh start. What are you going to do today or what did you do today to refresh yourself? Here's a few examples go on a bike ride, go for a walk, talk to a loved one or just enjoy your day. We all need a day to refresh our mind, body and soul.

_____
_____
_____
_____
_____
_____
_____
_____
_____

Isaiah 40:31 But they who wait for the Lord shall renew their strength; they shall mount up with wings like eagles; they shall run and not be weary; they shall walk and not faint.

There is more required of you.

Day 23 Require

Definition: 1. Need for a particular purpose. 2. Cause to be necessary.

There's more that's required from you today. No more mediocracy, no more average, but moving in the spirit of excellence. God is going to require you to do more if you want to gain more. You can't expect to move forward without placing requirements in your life for others to follow. Having requirements let others know what you want and what you expect from them and that's the same way God looks at us with his requirements for us.

What are you requiring today?

_____
_____
_____
_____
_____
_____
_____
_____
_____

Luke 12:48 Unto whomsoever much is given, of him shall be much required.

You reap what you sow.

Day 24 Reap

Definition: 1. Cut or gather (a crop or harvest). 2. Receive (a reward or benefit) as a consequence of one's own or other people's actions.

What's in your garden? You want to reap good things, but have you placed good seeds in fertile soil. Today begin to reflect what you are reaping. It's not too late to change your harvest to good. Begin to think of the good things you can do and say to begin to sow good seeds. Remember, you reap what you sow.

What are you sowing today?

_____
_____
_____
_____
_____
_____
_____
_____
_____
_____

Galatians 6:9 And let us not be weary in well doing: for in due season we shall reap if we faint not.

LIVE life with no regrets!

Day 25 Regrets

Definition: 1. feel sad, repentant, or disappointed over (something that has happened or been done, especially a loss or missed opportunity). 2. Used in polite formulas to express apology for or sadness over something unfortunate or unpleasant.

I know, I know life didn't go the way you might have thought and planned, but don't live in regrets. Yes, there were some mistakes made and maybe somethings you could have done better but still don't live in regrets. What you can do today don't put off until tomorrow because when you do it today, it releases the "I wish I did" and "I wish I could have" conversation. No more regrets, just actions!

Today release the REGRETS and begin to live now!

_____
_____
_____
_____
_____
_____
_____
_____

Romans 8:28 And we know that for those who love God all things work together for good, for those who are called according to his purpose.

You have to keep reaching.

Day 26 Reach

Definition: 1. Stretch out an arm in a specified direction in order to touch or grasp something. 2. Arrive at; get as far as.

You've made it to Day 26 and can't give up now. You must stretch your faith and continue to work hard so you can reach your goals. Sometimes reaching can cause a little discomfort and move you from familiar places, but once you arrive at your destination, you then learn your reaching was not in vain.

What are you reaching for?

_____
_____
_____
_____
_____
_____
_____
_____
_____

"If you want to reach a goal, you must 'see the reaching' in your own mind before you actually arrive at your goal." – Zig Ziglar

Your battery is dead.

Day 27 Recharge

Definition: 1. Restore an electric charge to (a battery or a battery-operated device) by connecting it to a device that draws power from another source of electricity. **2.** Return to a normal state of mind or strength after a period of physical or mental exertion.

It's time to plug in, take a break, and get some juice. You have drained your mental, physical, natural, spiritual, and emotional body battery out. It's time to recharge yourself. Use today to recharge and get your energy back. Think about how you can recharge and prepare for the plugin.

_____
_____
_____
_____
_____
_____
_____
_____
_____
_____
_____
_____
_____
_____

"Recharge your BODY like you recharge your PHONE" – Jabrina Speaks

It's time to take out the trash.

Day 28 Remove

Definition: 1. Take (something) away or off from the position occupied. **2.** Eliminate or get rid of it.

Today you will remove everything that's holding you back from a better tomorrow. It is time to remove the mask! What has caused you to stay in one place? Has it been self-doubt, self-afflictions, or your self-consciousness? Maybe even family, friends, or your job has kept you back? Today let's take a stand and make the necessary removals. What are you ready to remove?

_____
_____
_____
_____
_____
_____
_____
_____
_____
_____
_____
_____

> Love yourself enough to remove yourself from anything that you know isn't good for you.
> LiveLifeHappy.com

"Everywhere else, we are someone else, but at home, we remove our masks."
– Matthew Desmond

Is it worth it?

Day 29 Rethink, Respond and Retaliate

Definition: Rethink 1. A reassessment, especially one that results in changes being made.

Respond 1. Say something in reply.

Retaliate 1. Make an attack or assault in return for a similar attack.

STOP right now and RETHINK your actions and while you are rethinking, think about how you could, should, and would RESPOND. Now that you have done those two things, ask yourself, is it or was it really necessary to RETALIATE?

Everything we go through doesn't need a response or a retaliation. It's not worth your energy. You've grown from that place so what you would have done you don't do anymore. Today think about a situation you've been through or going through and write down your new thought process, how you are going to respond (if needed) and if retaliation is necessary.

_____

_____

_____

_____

_____

_____

"Rethink before you Respond because a Retaliation is not needed." – Jabrina Speaks

There's resilience in your blood type.

Day 30 Resilience/ Reaffirm

Definition: 1. (of a person or animal) Able to withstand or recover quickly from difficult conditions. 2. (of a substance or object) Able to recoil or spring back into shape after bending, stretching, or being compressed.

Over the course of life, you've had to bend, but you didn't break. You've had to stretch, but it only got you into shape. You've been compressed like a lemon but was able to make lemonade in the end. In other words, you have Resilience in your blood type. Life situation has reaffirmed that for you. By now, you didn't think you'll make it, but guess what you are here now.

Today, write yourself a letter reaffirming how resilience is in your blood type.

_____
_____
_____
_____
_____
_____
_____

"I do believe there's a heaven. I do believe that God has given me the resilience and survival skills to withstand the chiffon trenches." – Andre Leon Talley

You've made it!!

Day 31 Reflect, Review and Reinforce

Definition: Reflect 1. To prevent passage of and cause to change direction

Review 1. A general survey (as of the events of a period)

Reinforce 1. Strengthen or support

You have made it, WOW Day 31! You have done an amazing job and should be proud of yourself. Day 1 let us know it was okay to restart, Day 9 asked us to release some things, Day 27 told us to recharge ourselves and now Day 31 would like you to review, reflect and reinforce. Just that simple. Review each word, Reflect how you've grown and Reinforce them when needed. You've been on a journey these last 31 days and YOU MADE IT!

Write yourself a note of how PROUD you are of YOU!

_____
_____
_____
_____
_____
_____
_____
_____

"Your made it" Jabrina Speaks

Contact Information:

Jabrina Speaks

Email @ jabrinaspeaks@gmail.com

Facebook: @JabrinaThompson

Instagram: @Jabrinaspeaks

Website: www.jabrinaspeaks.us

Facebook: Jabrina Speaks

Interested in Writing and/or Publishing a Book?
Visit www.a2zbookspublishing.net

www.ingramcontent.com/pod-product-compliance
Lightning Source LLC
Chambersburg PA
CBHW052122110526
44592CB00013B/1715